Mophead hydrangeas.

Purple Pershore plums.

# Sue Kent

## Garden Notes

*Happy Gardening!*
*Sue Kent*

GRAFFEG

# Contents

Right: Oxeye daisies.

# Contents

# Garden Notes

**Good record-keeping makes for more successful gardening. We all think we will remember what we did where and when but if you are like me, it all seems a blur as the new year comes around.**

A handy aide mémoire of information combined with an efficient method of record-keeping takes the guesswork out of gardening tasks and enables the gardener to develop and build on successes and learn from any unsuccessful plantings and projects.

For me, learning is all about trial and error – by recording what I sow and plant and the mistakes I invariably make, I keep on track to become a better gardener. I made *Garden Notes* for personal use, as I could not find a book on the market that suited my needs. It is designed to be light in the hand, easy to read and use to record. It will fit any standard bookshelf and has a water-resistant cover that can be wiped for use outside. I thought fellow gardeners might find it useful too.

Included are sections on gardening, planning and many other things I find useful to know and record that normally get scribbled on the back of an envelope and promptly mislaid.

In *Garden Notes* there are reference charts for vegetable seed sowing, together with an area for seed sowing record-keeping, as well as identification assistance and advice for plant health problems, soil nutrition deficiencies and pest damage to save you wasting precious gardening time researching. There is also a place to record perennial and bulb planting activity so that you know where everything is when all is dormant.

# Garden Notes

I have provided a handy general pruning timings guide and an area to list plants in the garden that need annual pruning, with space to record if and when this has been done.

Also included are tips on storing garden produce, harvesting fresh flowers for indoor displays and drying as well as basic information for maintaining hand tools.

Helpful conversion charts and graph paper will assist you with garden design plans and visualising ideas and layouts. Nothing is date sensitive, so write as and when suits you.

In my previous life as a remedial massage therapist I dealt with many injuries caused by overenthusiastic gardening so in the last section of the book I have included advice and easy exercises with diagrams to keep the reader gardening safely for longer. There are note areas to record books to read, gifts to give and receive, wish list shopping lists, gardens to visit, and supplier's details together with pages to make up your own headings.

I have been recording my gardening activities and thoughts for 30 years, a beautiful history of effort and pleasure. I hope this notebook captures some of your efforts and in years to come you will look back at it and reflect on your gardening years.

**Happy Gardening**

Left: *Helenium* 'Waltraut'.

# Vegetables

**There is nothing like home-grown produce, and no matter what size garden you have, there is always space for growing some veg.**

**Beans and cucumbers can grow vertically and save space, onions and celery can hide in the flower border, lettuce will grow in a pot, and potatoes will grow in a bigger pot!**

I can't claim to be a master grower but I have found that some information can be quite helpful.

Understanding the plant family is useful, as they share the same flowering and fruiting behaviours and the majority grow well in the same soil conditions. I have included a table of vegetable plant families together with a crop rotation plan.

Rotating a vegetable crop helps with soil health and prevents pest proliferation and disease build up in the soil. Some vegetables also help others, for example, the legume family put nitrogen into the soil ready for brassicas to access it during the next season.

A vegetable growing area may not be big enough to use crop rotation. At the allotment I can rotate my crop, and at home I am lucky enough to have access to manure to refresh my soil, allowing me to grow many things in the same location every year. I apply a top dressing of manure in the autumn to prepare the soil for the spring.

The one exception are brassicas. These need to be grown on a different site every year, because they exhaust the soil more than any other crop, and if on the same site are liable to contract clubroot.

I'm frightfully forgetful, and cannot remember how far apart to plant my vegetables, so I've done some research and have provided what appear to be the standard vegetable spacing guidelines.

# Vegetables: Plant Families

This is a handy reminder of vegetable plant families, if using a crop rotation system.

**Chenopodiaceae**
**Beetroot family**
Beetroot
Good King Henry
Quinoa
Spinach
Swiss chard
Spinach beet

**Solanaceace**
**Potato family**
Aubergine
Pepper
Potato
Chilli

**Umbelliferae**
*(Apiaceae)*
**Carrot family**
Carrot
Celeriac
Celery
Fennel
Parsley
Parsnip
Tomato

**Alliaceae**
**Onion family**
Garlic
Leek
Onion
Shallot

**Cucurbitaceae**
**Marrow family**
Cucumber
Courgette
Marrow
Melon
Pumpkin
Squash

**Leguminosae**
*(Fabaceae)*
**Pea and bean family**
Alfalfa
Broad bean
French bean
Runner bean
Clover
Fenugreek
Pea

**Cruciferae**
*(Brassicaceae)*
**Cabbage family**
Broccoli
Brussels sprouts
Cabbage
Calabrese
Cauliflower
Kale
Kohlrabi
Mustard
Oriental brassicas
Radish

**Miscellaneous**
Corn
Lamb's lettuce
Miner's lettuce
New Zealand spinach
Purslane
Phacelia
Grazing rye
Buckwheat

# Vegetables: Crop Rotation

| Year 1 | Year 2 |
|---|---|
| **Bed A** | |
| Potatoes | Overwintered onions |
| Tomatoes | *Onion family* |
| | Peas and beans |
| | *Legume family* |
| **Bed B** | |
| Overwintered onions | Cabbage family |
| *Onion family* | *Apply compost in spring/* |
| Peas and beans | *summer* |
| *Legume family* | |
| **Bed C** | |
| Cabbage Family | Root vegetables |
| *Apply compost in spring/* | *Carrot family* |
| *summer* | Lettuce |
| | Swiss chard |
| | Spinach |
| **Bed D** | |
| Root vegetables | Potatoes |
| *Carrot family* | Tomatoes |
| Lettuce | |
| Swiss chard | |
| Spinach | |

# Vegetables: Crop Rotation

| Year 3 | Year 4 |
|---|---|
| **Bed A** | |
| Cabbage Family | Root vegetables |
| *Apply compost in spring/ summer* | *Carrot family* |
| | Lettuce |
| | Swiss chard |
| | Spinach |
| **Bed B** | |
| Root Vegetables | Potatoes |
| *Carrot family* | Tomatoes |
| Lettuce | |
| Swiss chard | |
| Spinach | |
| **Bed C** | |
| Potatoes | Overwintered onions |
| Tomatoes | *Onion family* |
| | Peas and beans |
| | *Legume family* |
| **Bed D** | |
| Overwintered onions | Cabbage family |
| *Onion family* | *Apply compost in spring/ summer* |
| Peas and beans | |
| *Legume family* | |

Information kindly provided by Garden Organic.

# Vegetables: Spacing

Vegetable spacing does not have to be prescriptive, however, following the guidelines in the charts provided should give the plants the best opportunity to be healthy and grow well, providing them with space to grow and enough ventilation to prevent pest damage and diseases.

Weeds growing between plants can remove vital nutrients from the soil and it's beneficial to remove them regularly before they get too big. Leaving enough space between rows makes weeding easier, and I cannot stress how beneficial regular weeding is – when I don't do it, my crop is compromised, and when I do, the rewards are great. Thinning out the seedlings, so plants are spaced correctly may seem harsh, but will allow the remaining plants room to develop strongly. This is my least enjoyable task, but again, one that ensures a good, healthy crop.

I grow many of my vegetables in containers using a soil mix of half manure and half compost, which is very rich (not the standard recommended mix). I plant the vegetables closer together than recommended, as they have a lot of food at their disposal, and this also makes the most of growing in a small space. In theory the plants are at risk from lack of ventilation and, depending on how close they are planted, may not develop to their full size, but for me, so far so good.

Right: Celery harvesting.

# Vegetables: Spacing

| Vegetable | Between Plants | | Between Rows | |
|---|---|---|---|---|
| | Inches | Centimetres | Inches | Centimetres |
| Artichokes | 18" | 45cm | 24"– 36" | 60-90cm |
| Asparagus | 12" – 18" | 30-45cm | 60" | 150cm |
| Aubergine | 18" – 24" | 45-60cm | 30" – 36" | 75-91cm |
| Beans Bush | 2" – 4" | 5-10cm | 18" – 24" | 45-60cm |
| Beans – Climbing | 4" – 6" | 10-15cm | 30" – 36" | 75-90cm |
| Beetroot | 3" – 4" | 7.5-10cm | 12" – 18" | 30-45cm |
| Bok Choy | 6" – 12" | 15-30cm | 18" – 30" | 45-75cm |
| Broccoli | 18" – 24" | 45-60cm | 36" – 40" | 75-100cm |
| Brussels Sprouts | 24" | 50cm | 24" – 36" | 60-90cm |
| Cabbage | 9" – 12" | 23-30cm | 36" – 44" | 90-112cm |
| Carrots | 1" – 2" | 2.5-5cm | 12" – 18" | 30-45cm |
| Cauliflower | 18" – 24" | 45-60cm | 18" – 24" | 45-60cm |
| Celery | 12" – 18" | 30-45cm | 24" | 60cm |
| Corn | 10" – 15" | 25-38cm | 36" – 42" | 90-106cm |
| Courgette | 24" – 36" | 60-90cm | 36" – 48" | 90-120cm |
| Cucumbers | 12" | 30cm | 30" | 75cm |
| Fennel Bulb | 12" – 24" | 30-60cm | 12" – 24" | 30-60cm |
| Kohlrabi | 6" | 15cm | 12" | 30cm |
| Leeks | 4" – 6" | 10-15cm | 8" – 16" | 20-40cm |
| Lettuce Head | 12" | 30cm | 12" | 30cm |
| Onions | 4" – 6" | 10-15cm | 4" – 6" | 10-15cm |
| Parsnips | 8" – 10" | 20-25cm | 18" – 24" | 45-60cm |
| Peppers | 14" – 18" | 35-45cm | 18" – 24" | 45-60cm |
| Peas | 1"-2" | 2.5-5cm | 18" – 24" | 45-60cm |
| Potatoes | 8" – 12" | 20-30cm | 30" – 36" | 75-90cm |
| Pumpkins | 60" – 72" | 1.5-1.8m | 120" – 180" | 3-4.5m |
| Radicchio | 8" – 10" | 20-25cm | 12" | 18cm |
| Radishes | 1" – 2" | 2.5- 5cm | 2" – 4" | 5-10cm |
| Rhubarb | 36" – 48" | 90-120cm | 36" – 48" | 90-120cm |
| Salsify | 2" – 4" | 5-10cm | 18" – 20" | 45-50cm |
| Shallots | 6" – 8" | 15-20cm | 6" – 8" | 15-20cm |
| Spinach | 2" – 4" | 5-10cm | 12" – 18" | 30-45cm |
| Sweed | 8" – 10" | 20– 25cm | 14" – 18" | 34-45cm |
| Swiss Chard | 6" – 12" | 15-30cm | 12" – 18" | 30-45cm |
| Tomatoes | 24" – 36" | 60-90cm | 48" – 60" | 90-150cm |
| Turnips | 3" – 6" | 7.5-15cm | 12" – 18" | 30-45cm |

# Seed Germination

**Different seeds require different temperatures to get started, and understanding germination temperatures and timescales is helpful in avoiding failure. The reference table provided will help guide timings for seed sowing.**

Keep a record in this book when the seeds are sown. This will help you to see if they germinate in the expected time, while in the comments box you can record how they develop and if they're worth growing again, useful for the current year and as a reference for future years.

Buying seeds and raising a plant takes money, time and effort. Recording how they perform will guide and educate your future flower and vegetable purchases and growing efforts.

I have a tendency to want to get everything underway early in the season on my windowsills. I have in the past sowed my cucumbers and beans and some annual flowers far too early, inflicting needless disappointment, but I have learned!

Below: Storing seeds in a cool, dry place.

# Seed Germination Temperatures and Timescales

| | Minimum | | Optimum | | Maximum | | Approximate days to germination at optimal temp |
|---|---|---|---|---|---|---|---|
| | Min °F | Min °C | Opt °F | Opt °C | Max °F | Max °C | |
| Asparagus | 50 | 10 | 60-85 | 16-29 | 95 | 35 | 14-18 |
| Aubergine | 60 | 16 | 75-85 | 24-29 | 95 | 35 | 10-15 |
| Bean, broad | 42 | 5 | 46-59 | 10-14 | 82 | 28 | 8-15 |
| Bean, French | 46 | 8 | 60-85 | 16-30 | 95 | 35 | 7 |
| Bean, runner | 46 | 8 | 60-85 | 16-30 | 95 | 35 | 7 |
| Beetroot | 40 | 4 | 60-85 | 16-29 | 80 | 27 | 4-10 |
| Broccoli | 40 | 4 | 60-85 | 16-29 | 95 | 35 | 7-10 |
| Brussels sprouts | 40 | 4 | 60-85 | 16-29 | 95 | 35 | 3-10 |
| Cabbage | 40 | 4 | 60-85 | 16-29 | 95 | 35 | 4-10 |
| Carrot | 40 | 4 | 65-85 | 18-29 | 95 | 35 | 6 |
| Celery | 40 | 4 | 60-70 | 16-21 | 95 | 35 | 10 |
| Cabbage | 40 | 4 | 60-85 | 16-29 | 95 | 35 | 5-10 |
| Cauliflower | 40 | 4 | 60-85 | 16-29 | 95 | 35 | 8-10 |
| Courgette | 55 | 3 | 65-75 | 18-24 | 75 | 25 | 7-10 |
| Corn | 50 | 10 | 65-95 | 18-35 | 105 | 41 | 4-10 |
| Cucumber | 60 | 16 | 65-95 | 18-35 | 105 | 41 | 5-7 |
| Endive | 35 | 2 | 60-75 | 16-24 | 85 | 29 | 10-14 |
| Garlic | 35 | 2 | 65-85 | 18-29 | 95 | 35 | 7-14 |
| Kale | 40 | 4 | 60-85 | 16-29 | 95 | 35 | 5-7 |
| Kohlrabi | 40 | 4 | 60-95 | 16-35 | 105 | 41 | 5-10 |
| Leeks | 35 | 2 | 65-85 | 18-29 | 95 | 35 | 8-16 |
| Lettuce | 35 | 2 | 60-75 | 16-24 | 85 | 29 | 2-10 |
| Onion | 35 | 2 | 65-85 | 18-29 | 95 | 35 | 4-12 |
| Parsley | 40 | 4 | 65-85 | 18-29 | 95 | 35 | 10-25 |
| Parsnip | 35 | 2 | 65-75 | 18-24 | 85 | 29 | 5-28 |
| Pea | 40 | 4 | 65-75 | 18-24 | 85 | 29 | 5-7 |
| Pepper | 60 | 16 | 65-75 | 18-24 | 95 | 35 | 7-10 |
| Pumpkin | 60 | 16 | 85-95 | 29-35 | 105 | 41 | 4-10 |
| Radish | 40 | 4 | 65-85 | 18-29 | 95 | 35 | 4-10 |
| Spinach | 35 | 2 | 65-75 | 18-24 | 75 | 24 | 6-14 |
| Squash | 60 | 16 | 85-95 | 29-35 | 105 | 41 | 7-10 |
| Swiss chard | 40 | 4 | 65-85 | 18-29 | 95 | 35 | 7.00 |
| Tomato | 50 | 10 | 65-85 | 18-29 | 95 | 35 | 5-7 |
| Turnip | 40 | 4 | 60-95 | 16-35 | 105 | 41 | 3-10 |

# Flower and Vegetable

| Date | Seed type | Variety |
|------|-----------|---------|
|      |           |         |
|      |           |         |
|      |           |         |
|      |           |         |
|      |           |         |
|      |           |         |
|      |           |         |
|      |           |         |
|      |           |         |
|      |           |         |
|      |           |         |
|      |           |         |
|      |           |         |
|      |           |         |
|      |           |         |
|      |           |         |
|      |           |         |
|      |           |         |
|      |           |         |
|      |           |         |

# Seed Sowing Record

**Supplier**

**Comment**

# Flower and Vegetable

| Date | Seed type | Variety |
|------|-----------|---------|
|      |           |         |
|      |           |         |
|      |           |         |
|      |           |         |
|      |           |         |
|      |           |         |
|      |           |         |
|      |           |         |
|      |           |         |
|      |           |         |
|      |           |         |
|      |           |         |
|      |           |         |
|      |           |         |
|      |           |         |
|      |           |         |
|      |           |         |
|      |           |         |
|      |           |         |
|      |           |         |
|      |           |         |

# Seed Sowing Record

**Supplier**

**Comment**

# Flower and Vegetable

| Date | Seed type | Variety |
|------|-----------|---------|
|      |           |         |
|      |           |         |
|      |           |         |
|      |           |         |
|      |           |         |
|      |           |         |
|      |           |         |
|      |           |         |
|      |           |         |
|      |           |         |
|      |           |         |
|      |           |         |
|      |           |         |
|      |           |         |
|      |           |         |
|      |           |         |
|      |           |         |
|      |           |         |
|      |           |         |
|      |           |         |

# Seed Sowing Record

| Supplier | Comment |
| --- | --- |
| | |
| | |
| | |
| | |
| | |
| | |
| | |
| | |
| | |
| | |
| | |
| | |
| | |
| | |
| | |
| | |
| | |
| | |
| | |
| | |
| | |
| | |
| | |
| | |
| | |
| | |

# Flower and Vegetable

| Date | Seed type | Variety |
|------|-----------|---------|
|      |           |         |
|      |           |         |
|      |           |         |
|      |           |         |
|      |           |         |
|      |           |         |
|      |           |         |
|      |           |         |
|      |           |         |
|      |           |         |
|      |           |         |
|      |           |         |
|      |           |         |
|      |           |         |
|      |           |         |
|      |           |         |
|      |           |         |
|      |           |         |
|      |           |         |

# Seed Sowing Record

**Supplier**

**Comment**

# Flower and Vegetable

| Date | Seed type | Variety |
|------|-----------|---------|
|  |  |  |
|  |  |  |
|  |  |  |
|  |  |  |
|  |  |  |
|  |  |  |
|  |  |  |
|  |  |  |
|  |  |  |
|  |  |  |
|  |  |  |
|  |  |  |
|  |  |  |
|  |  |  |
|  |  |  |
|  |  |  |
|  |  |  |
|  |  |  |
|  |  |  |
|  |  |  |
|  |  |  |

# Seed Sowing Record

**Supplier**

**Comment**

# Plant Health

**I often need to refer to general information on plant health when facing simple problems in the garden. This section will help you to identify and resolve common plant health issues and the different areas that can help or hinder healthy plant development.**

Being so variable, climate is the factor we have the least control over! Plants can often suffer setbacks, with those grown in containers particularly susceptible to damage. Understanding a plant's natural habitat will help guide the location it will be best suited to in your garden and avoid some common weather-related problems. Putting the right plant in the right place is key to success. There is more about this in the design section of this book.

Plant nutrition is a complex subject. Like humans, plants need good nutrition to thrive – healthy soil is the key to healthy plant life. To help diagnose possible plant deficiencies, I have created a table with the most common nutrients plants require, the benefits they provide and how to spot possible deficiencies.

I suggest ways to enrich the soil and feed the plants, how to make liquid plant feeds for their short-term nutritional needs and how to use resources from within the garden to enrich the soil's long-term health. This is a natural approach with the added benefit of saving loads of money!

The last part of this section looks at some common pest problems, how to spot them and how to deal with them. I have to admit, living in wet Wales, the slugs win, and I have given up trying to grow certain flowering plants. It makes my gardening activities easier and more enjoyable to choose flowers the slug will ignore.

Left: Hebe rescued from a skip.

# Plant Health

## Weather-related Problems and Causes

| Problem | Common Cause |
| --- | --- |
| Blackened leaves | Frost damage. |
| Scorched foliage (drying from leaf tips inwards) | Direct hot sun. Windy or dry conditions. |
| Ragged foliage | Heavy winds, rain or hail. The plant is now more vulnerable to disease. |
| Wind rock/root rock (can occur with recently planted, unsecured trees and shrubs) | Fierce winds. Top heavy plants. Compacted soil in the surrounding area. |
| Wilting | A lack of soil moisture. |
| | Soil that's too wet. |
| | Shut-down response to extreme heat. |
| | Newly transplanted seedlings and other plants that have recently been moved outdoors. |

# Plant Health

## Suggested Action

- Don't remove damaged foliage until the threat of frost has passed. The plant should recover and show new growth.

- In dry weather, apply water to roots, not leaves. In windy or sunny conditions, consider moving the plant to offer natural protection and shade.

- Remove damaged foliage. In most cases the leaves will be quickly replaced.

- Stake the plant. The stake height is advised at no more than one-third of stem height.
- If and when suitable, prune back leggy stems and create an open framework.
- Fork over the soil at the outer edge of the root ball.

- Check to see if moist to a depth of at least 6"/15cm for most vegetable plants and other annuals. If not water well.

- Stop supplemental watering and wait for the soil to dry out.

- Wait to see if the plants recover in the evening when temperatures cool.

- Place in a lightly shaded, wind-protected area or cover them with garden fabric until acclimatised.

# Plant Nutrition

**Plant nutrition plays a crucial role in the growth and development of plants. A fundamental aspect is soil pH, which affects nutrient absorption. Conducting a soil pH test helps determine the soil type, with most vegetable plants thriving in a pH of around 6.8. Incorrect pH levels can hinder nutrient uptake even if they are present in the soil.**

Fertilisers are vital tools for supplying essential nutrients to plants. They often contain compounds rich in nitrogen, phosphorus and potassium, known as NPK fertilisers. These nutrients support various aspects of plant growth. Nitrogen aids in leaf and stem development, phosphorus contributes to root growth and flower production, while potassium enhances overall plant health and disease resistance.

Organic fertilisers offer a more natural approach, providing a diverse range of slow-release nutrients along with micronutrients. These fertilisers contribute to soil health and microbial activity, fostering a sustainable growth environment. Unlike synthetic fertilisers that can cause nutrient imbalances and harm the ecosystem, organic options improve soil structure and long-term fertility.

Left: *Allium nutans.*

# Plant Nutrition

Sometimes plants need a helping hand. They give clues to the help they need. Check the chart to help read the signs.

| Nutrient | Benefit |
| --- | --- |
| Nitrogen | Plant growth. |
| Phosphorus | Seed germination, roots and fruits. |
| Potassium | Osmotic regulator.<br>Protects from frost damage.<br>General plant health. |
| Magnesium | Helps uptake of phosphorus. |
| Calcium | Healthy cell structure and roots. |
| Sulphur | Assists in the synthesis of chlorophyll. |
| Iron and Manganese | Assists in the synthesis of chlorophyll. |

# Plant Nutrition

## Deficiency

- Slow spindly growth.
- Yellowing of leaves (older ones first).
- Stems may be red or purple.
- Reduction of root and stem development.
- Darkening of leaves.
- Brown leaf patches.
- Brown scorched patches on older leaf tips and margins.
- Leaves may bronze and roll inwards and downwards.

- Loss of green in the leaves, leading to reddening and eventual death.

- Inwardly curling, pale young leaves.
- May cause leaves to die at growing point.

- Loss of green in young leaves.

- Loss of green colour in the interveinal part of younger leaves.

# Plant Nutrition: Common Feeds

## Compost

A slow-release natural fertiliser containing phosphorus, nitrogen and potassium, compost also improves soil texture.

For a circular system of gardening, make your own compost from kitchen scraps, garden waste, lawn clippings and ripped up cardboard. The smaller the waste size, the quicker it will rot and make compost, so chop up any large material before adding it to the compost heap or container. Layer the types of waste, and resist putting a large amount of any one thing in on its own. Layering the heap and turning once a month will make it compost faster, and turning it twice a month even faster still!

To kill weed seed, compost temperatures need to reach 50°C/112°F. If your compost heap does not get to the correct temperature, make sure to remove any unwanted seedlings that develop where the compost is used as soon as they appear to prevent them establishing and taking nutrients away from the plants. Compost is ready when it is dark brown, feels crumbly like soil and smells like damp woodland.

## Animal Manure

Manures are high in nitrogen and can be bought bagged or sourced directly from some farms. Rabbit and chicken pellets have the highest nutrient content but do not add texture to the soil, only food. Cow and horse manure have little difference in their nutrient content. Horse takes the longest to rot down and provides more texture.

Horse and cow manure need to be well rotted, as the high concentration of nitrate in its fresh state can burn the plant's roots, as I know to my cost.

# Plant Nutrition: Common Feeds

Spread raw manure on empty vegetable beds in the autumn when at least 120 days will pass before an edible crop will be produced. As the manure mixes with soil, the soil microorganisms clear out the residual waste's bacteria.

## Bone Meal

Bone meal is a slow-release fertiliser that is high in phosphorus, low in nitrogen and also contains calcium. Add a small amount of bone meal as directed on the packaging to alleviate a phosphorus deficiency. Use gloves to apply to the top of the soil or add to compost when planting, mixing well to avoid root burn.

## Homemade Comfrey Liquid Feed

Comfrey feed is made from the leaves of the comfrey plant. A liquid comfrey feed has a higher NPK ratio than farmyard manure. Comfrey also contains vitamin B12, so it's a rich source of food for plants. Comfrey leaves are hairy and can cause skin irritation, so wear long sleeves and gloves when making this.

- Cut them before flowering and leave to wilt for a day to reduce their moisture content.

- Fill a bucket with a lid with comfrey leaves, packed in as tightly as possible and weighed down with a brick or stone, then add enough water to cover and place the lid on.

- Leave this for two weeks in warm weather, or four weeks in cold weather.

- As the comfrey decomposes, it smells horrid, so place somewhere where it will not cause any moaning!

- Strain into a clean bucket, then pour into an airtight container.

# Plant Nutrition: Common Feeds

- Label it clearly and keep out of children's reach, using within the season in which it has been made.

To use: dilute 1 part comfrey to 10 parts water, or until it looks like tea. It is not suitable for young plants, so apply only to established plants with good root systems. Like tomato feed, it can encourage a good crop of fruits and veg and also be used on roses.

The soggy comfrey strained from the feed can be used as a mulch for potatoes or tomatoes or on the compost heap. French and runner beans will benefit from comfrey in the planting trench or when applied as a mulch.

## Homemade Nettle Feed

Nettle feed is made in the same way as comfrey: dilute 1 part feed to 10 parts water for watering plants or 1:20 for direct foliar application. Protect your skin from raw nettles and keep away from your face – they are called stinging nettles for a reason.

Plants like tomatoes and roses do not enjoy the high iron levels in nettle fertiliser. Use for feeding leafy plants and heavy feeders.

# Plant Nutrition: Common Feeds

## Homemade Leaf Mould

Leaf mould does not contain many nutrients but is good for sowing seedlings or as a mulch to protect plants and improve soil structure.

Collect fallen leaves and put them into a container with lots of aeration to rot down – I use an old mesh laundry basket, but equally good is a wooden frame with chicken wire, old builders' sacks, hessian sacks or a plastic bag with holes.

One-year-old leaf mould is suitable for mulching, soil improving and for autumn top dressing for lawns, while two-year-old leaf mould is suitable for sowing seeds. Use on its own or mix with equal parts sharp sand to make a perfect low-nutrient medium for seed germination.

For potting mix, adding comfrey leaves to autumn leaves can increase the leaf mould's nutrient content. Adding grass cuttings will increase the nitrate content.

## Homemade Potting Mix

To make a homemade potting mix, combine 1/3 garden compost, 1/3 sharp sand and 1/3 well-rotted leaf mould.

Left: Romaine lettuce seedlings.

# Pests & Predators

**I try to garden using organic principles and these include encouraging biodiversity to achieve a healthy interdependence between plants and wildlife.**

I don't use toxic chemicals to kill weeds, diseases and pests as they can damage my health, the health of my garden and all the lifeforms within and beyond it.

It requires patience and knowledge to create this harmony between nature and a thriving garden, and means taking an interest in wildlife and identifying common pests that may damage crops, like slugs, blackfly and cabbage white butterflies. Understanding their life cycles can help to manage the problems they can cause. Knowing when to expect them, I can plan companion planting and use physical barriers like fleece or netting to deter them. However, for me, the easiest way of keeping my plants healthy is to physically remove the pests and to encourage their predators, like ladybirds, hedgehogs and frogs, to remove them for me.

To help me learn the complexities of nature 30 years ago, I became a member of Garden Organic, an organisation dedicated to gardening within natural systems and cycles, making the best use of resources and avoiding harmful chemicals. They have provided super organic gardening support and advice.

Keeping a record of what is living with you in your garden can give you a wider understanding of how to plant to encourage a balanced, healthy environment. Record what you will – birds, insects, reptiles and mammals all have their role to play.

I am on a mission to encourage the peacock butterfly into my garden, so am planning to increase the plants in my garden it likes to visit. You may want to see a particular visitor in your garden. The Wildlife Trust has great information to help you do just that: **www.wildlifetrusts.org**.

# Pests & Predators: Garlic Spray

I use organic methods, and here is my recipe for garlic spray insect and slug deterrent.

**Garlic spray ingredients**

1 bulb of garlic and 1 litre of water.

## Method

- Put the whole garlic bulb into the water, boil until soft, then mash the clove with a fork and leave to cool.

- Remove the garlic using a sieve and keep the water in a sealed bottle.

- To use, dilute one tablespoon to two litres of water. Put this into a sprayer or spray bottle and use weekly on leaves, under and over, and repeat if raining.

- Use to deter aphids, chewing insects and cabbage white butterflies. I use it on hostas and young leafy greens to deter slugs.

Below: Cabbage white butterfly.

# Pests & Predators

| Pest Damage | Culprit |
| --- | --- |
| **Missing seedlings and nibbled leaves.** | Slugs, active mostly at night and in damp conditions. |
| **Ragged holes in leaves.** | Caterpillars. |
| **Clusters of soft-bodied green or black creatures covering a part of the plant.** | Blackfly and greenfly. |
| **Small round holes in seedlings and young plants.** | Flea beetles. |

**Visit Garden Organic for more ideas and information:**
www.gardenorganic.org.uk

| Action | Predators |
|---|---|
| • Clear vegetation from the immediate area.<br>• Go out at night with a torch and remove them.<br>• Put a physical barrier up – cloches from plastic bottles are quick and easy.<br>• Make garlic spray (see page 45) or beer traps. | • Black scuttling ground beetle.<br>• Centipedes.<br>• Frogs, toads and hedgehogs. |
| • Pick them off by hand while still small. | • Birds, wasps, parasitic flies, ground beetles and spiders will apparently eat caterpillars. |
| • Squash colonies of pests with your fingers, if this can be achieved without damaging the plant.<br>• Pinch infested tops out of broad beans.<br>• As a last resort, use insecticidal soap or rape seed oil from garden centres or mail order. | • Wait for the ladybirds, lacewings and hoverflies to arrive and eat the blackfly and greenfly – trust and they will come. |
| • Water well to encourage strong growth and they should outgrow the damage. | • Birds, frogs and ground beetles. |

# Pests & Predators: Wildlife Record

| Date | Name | Location | Weather |
|------|------|----------|---------|
|      |      |          |         |
|      |      |          |         |
|      |      |          |         |
|      |      |          |         |
|      |      |          |         |
|      |      |          |         |
|      |      |          |         |
|      |      |          |         |
|      |      |          |         |
|      |      |          |         |
|      |      |          |         |
|      |      |          |         |
|      |      |          |         |
|      |      |          |         |
|      |      |          |         |
|      |      |          |         |
|      |      |          |         |
|      |      |          |         |
|      |      |          |         |
|      |      |          |         |
|      |      |          |         |

# Pests & Predators: Wildlife Record

| Date | Name | Location | Weather |
|------|------|----------|---------|
|      |      |          |         |
|      |      |          |         |
|      |      |          |         |
|      |      |          |         |
|      |      |          |         |
|      |      |          |         |
|      |      |          |         |
|      |      |          |         |
|      |      |          |         |
|      |      |          |         |
|      |      |          |         |
|      |      |          |         |
|      |      |          |         |
|      |      |          |         |
|      |      |          |         |
|      |      |          |         |
|      |      |          |         |
|      |      |          |         |
|      |      |          |         |
|      |      |          |         |
|      |      |          |         |
|      |      |          |         |

# Plants & Bulbs

**For over 30 years I have kept a record of nearly every plant and bulb I have acquired for my garden. As time has gone by, I have realised the value of adding the additional information of recording where I put them.**

In the dormant months it's very difficult to see what's under the soil, and I found trying to recall what is there is a hit and miss affair. Referring to my *Garden Notes* record prevents me from damaging existing plants when putting new ones into the borders or planting bulbs in a position when there are some already there.

Keeping good records allows me to see how long a plant takes to develop into its full glory. With bulbs it shows me the longevity and multiplication of a bulb or if it is a dud or a one hit wonder. It also means I can remove labels and throw away packets!

This record-keeping helps me make complimentary selections that will harmonise with my existing garden design when purchasing new plants or bulbs.

My notes are a reminder of what thrives and what fails, directing my plant selections to create resilience in the garden. Most importantly, putting it down on paper frees up space in my brain for other things. There is only so much information one can keep in one's head.

Left: Autumn mixed bulb planting.

# Plants & Bulbs: Buying & Planting

| Date | Plant | Location |
|------|-------|----------|
|      |       |          |
|      |       |          |
|      |       |          |
|      |       |          |
|      |       |          |
|      |       |          |
|      |       |          |
|      |       |          |
|      |       |          |
|      |       |          |
|      |       |          |
|      |       |          |
|      |       |          |
|      |       |          |
|      |       |          |
|      |       |          |
|      |       |          |
|      |       |          |
|      |       |          |
|      |       |          |
|      |       |          |
|      |       |          |

# Plants & Bulbs: Buying & Planting

| Date | Plant | Location |
|------|-------|----------|
|      |       |          |
|      |       |          |
|      |       |          |
|      |       |          |
|      |       |          |
|      |       |          |
|      |       |          |
|      |       |          |
|      |       |          |
|      |       |          |
|      |       |          |
|      |       |          |
|      |       |          |
|      |       |          |
|      |       |          |
|      |       |          |
|      |       |          |
|      |       |          |
|      |       |          |
|      |       |          |
|      |       |          |

# Plants & Bulbs: Buying & Planting

| Date | Plant | Location |
|------|-------|----------|
|      |       |          |
|      |       |          |
|      |       |          |
|      |       |          |
|      |       |          |
|      |       |          |
|      |       |          |
|      |       |          |
|      |       |          |
|      |       |          |
|      |       |          |
|      |       |          |
|      |       |          |
|      |       |          |
|      |       |          |
|      |       |          |
|      |       |          |
|      |       |          |
|      |       |          |
|      |       |          |

# Plants & Bulbs: Buying & Planting

| Date | Plant | Location |
|------|-------|----------|
|      |       |          |
|      |       |          |
|      |       |          |
|      |       |          |
|      |       |          |
|      |       |          |
|      |       |          |
|      |       |          |
|      |       |          |
|      |       |          |
|      |       |          |
|      |       |          |
|      |       |          |
|      |       |          |
|      |       |          |
|      |       |          |
|      |       |          |
|      |       |          |
|      |       |          |
|      |       |          |
|      |       |          |
|      |       |          |

# Plants & Bulbs: Buying & Planting

| Date | Plant | Location |
|------|-------|----------|
|      |       |          |
|      |       |          |
|      |       |          |
|      |       |          |
|      |       |          |
|      |       |          |
|      |       |          |
|      |       |          |
|      |       |          |
|      |       |          |
|      |       |          |
|      |       |          |
|      |       |          |
|      |       |          |
|      |       |          |
|      |       |          |
|      |       |          |
|      |       |          |
|      |       |          |
|      |       |          |

# Plants & Bulbs: Buying & Planting

| Date | Plant | Location |
| --- | --- | --- |
| | | |
| | | |
| | | |
| | | |
| | | |
| | | |
| | | |
| | | |
| | | |
| | | |
| | | |
| | | |
| | | |
| | | |
| | | |
| | | |
| | | |
| | | |
| | | |
| | | |
| | | |
| | | |
| | | |
| | | |
| | | |
| | | |
| | | |

# Notes

# Notes

# Notes

# Notes

# Notes

# Notes

# Notes

# Notes

# Notes

# Notes

# Pruning Tips

**Pruning is a skill – if you are unsure of when or how to prune, it is wise to spend time acquiring the relevant information. *Gardeners' World* Magazine and the RHS have general information online.**

Here are a few guidelines for when to prune common shrubs and trees. In the recording section you can make a note of shrubs and trees you have, any specific needs and timings and record if/when the task is carried out.

• Follow established pruning guidelines.

• Clean your pruning tools before and after each job to avoid spreading any disease.

• Look for dead, diseased or dying wood and remove it first.

• Remove crossing branches.

• Remove inward-facing branches.

For detailed pruning information, I recommend *Pruning: The RHS Encyclopedia of Practical Gardening*. An easier read for regenerative gardening is *Revive your Garden: How to Bring Your Outdoor Space Back to Life* by Nick Bailey.

Left: Deadheading roses with an ARS long-handled pruner.

# Pruning Tips

## Deciduous Trees and Shrubs

**Spring pruning (before flowering)**

- Plants that flower from July-October and are deciduous.

- Prune last year's growth to just two or three buds above healthy, thick stems to provide a good framework for new growth.

**Summer pruning (after flowering)**

- For plants that flower from November–June and are deciduous, prune immediately after flowering.

- Prune flowered stems back to a strong upright shoot, as low as possible. Remove older branches which flower weakly. Remove one stem in three e.g. a shrub with five stems would have the two largest and oldest shoots removed down to 25-45cm (10-18in) above the soil.

- **Evergreen trees and shrubs** – prune after flowering.

- Remove old flowers and cut back to healthy, outward-facing buds. Remove damaged, diseased or old and straggly growth. Take out stems and branches to improve congestion and balance the plant.

- **Newly planted trees and shrubs** – these should not need pruning for a few years.

# Pruning Tips

## Roses

- **Hybrid teas, floribunda, ground cover, shrub and miniature container roses** – prune late winter when growth is just starting.

- **Climbing** – (repeat flowering) prune in winter.

- **Rambling** – (flowers once, normally June) – prune late summer. Renovate in winter.

## Fruit

- **Blackberries and hybrid berries such as boysenberries loganberries** – cut back after fruiting around September.

- **Blackcurrants** – removing branches during harvest makes picking easier and prunes at the same time – what is not to love about that! Pruning can also be done in the winter.

- **Red and white currants** – prune in winter.

- **Summer-fruiting raspberries** – prune after fruiting and cut to ground level.

- **Autumn-fruiting raspberries** – cut back old canes to ground level in February.

- **Apples and pears trees** – prune during winter.

- **Trained apples and pears** – prune by the end of August.

- **Outdoor grapes** – pinch out new shoots during spring and summer and prune during early winter (later can cause the vine to bleed and weaken).

# Pruning Record

| Plant | Location | When to prune |
|-------|----------|---------------|
|       |          |               |
|       |          |               |
|       |          |               |
|       |          |               |
|       |          |               |
|       |          |               |
|       |          |               |
|       |          |               |
|       |          |               |
|       |          |               |
|       |          |               |
|       |          |               |
|       |          |               |
|       |          |               |
|       |          |               |
|       |          |               |
|       |          |               |
|       |          |               |
|       |          |               |
|       |          |               |
|       |          |               |
|       |          |               |

**Keep a note of the plants in the garden that need pruning, when they need it and what years they are pruned.**

| Plant | Location | When to prune |
| --- | --- | --- |
| | | |
| | | |
| | | |
| | | |
| | | |
| | | |
| | | |
| | | |
| | | |
| | | |
| | | |
| | | |
| | | |
| | | |
| | | |
| | | |
| | | |
| | | |
| | | |
| | | |
| | | |
| | | |
| | | |
| | | |

# Pruning Record

| Plant | Location | When to prune |
|-------|----------|---------------|
|       |          |               |
|       |          |               |
|       |          |               |
|       |          |               |
|       |          |               |
|       |          |               |
|       |          |               |
|       |          |               |
|       |          |               |
|       |          |               |
|       |          |               |
|       |          |               |
|       |          |               |
|       |          |               |
|       |          |               |
|       |          |               |
|       |          |               |
|       |          |               |
|       |          |               |
|       |          |               |
|       |          |               |
|       |          |               |

**Keep a note of the plants in the garden that need pruning, when they need it and what years they are pruned.**

| Plant | Location | When to prune |
|-------|----------|---------------|
|       |          |               |
|       |          |               |
|       |          |               |
|       |          |               |
|       |          |               |
|       |          |               |
|       |          |               |
|       |          |               |
|       |          |               |
|       |          |               |
|       |          |               |
|       |          |               |
|       |          |               |
|       |          |               |
|       |          |               |
|       |          |               |
|       |          |               |
|       |          |               |
|       |          |               |

# Storing Crops: Tips

**I love making the most of all my hard work, and storing crops prolongs the life of the fruit and vegetables grown.**

**Store only perfect crops in a rodent-free place, using damaged ones as soon as possible.**

## Herbs

- Cut herbs before they flower for the fullest flavour.
- Cut during the morning time, when the dew has dried from the leaves.
- Do not use yellowing leaves or leaves spotted with disease.
- Shake branches to remove any insects.
- Tie six or seven stems at a time.
- Hang or lay herbs in a warm, dry, ventilated space. I often use my attic and have a hanging rail in my shed.
- Remove no more than two-thirds of the plant's growth.
- When dried, check for any signs of mould and discard.
- Store dried in airtight containers that are dated and labelled.
- Place out of direct sunlight, in the dark where possible.

Left: Homegrown vegetables.

# Storing Crops: Tips

## Fruit

### Apples

- The earlier-maturing apples do not store well, mid-season apples store for about 4-5 weeks, while late-fruiting varieties usually last the longest.

- Pick from the tree in dry weather, early in the morning, when the fruit is cool.

- Store on trays in single layers in a dry, dark place. Arrange them so that they do not touch each other, or wrap individually in newspaper. Keep apples that ripen at different times separate.

- Store at a temperature of 2°C to 5°C.

### Pears

- Pick when still firm. Late-season varieties should not be picked too early to avoid them shrivelling. Store on slatted shelves in a single layer, unwrapped. Check frequently and bring into a warm room to finish the ripening process.

- Store at a temperature of 0°C to 1°C.

# Storing Crops: Tips

## Vegetables

Checked stored vegetables. Once they turn soft and/or start growing, compost them.

### Beans and peas

When growing beans and peas, pick the drying pods when they have darkened and are dry, before the pod starts to split – the beans should rattle inside. If they need further drying after shelling then lay them out in a single layer to dry on a sunny windowsill.

### Beetroot, carrots, celeriac, horseradish, kohlrabi, parsnip, turnip, swede and salsify

Harvest on a cool day or cool before storing. Twist off the leaves close to the crown, store in a dark, frost-free place in boxes of nearly dry sharp sand, leaf mould or sawdust (untreated wood only) in layers, not touching each other.

• Store at a temperature of 0°C to 4°C.

### Garlic

• Lift carefully, when the leaves have turned yellow. Bruising the bulb will reduce its storing ability. Delaying harvest may cause the bulbs to open and not store as well. Softneck garlic stores for longer than hardneck varieties. Dry in the sun (not over 30°C) or well-ventilated shed for 2-4 weeks, cut the dead stalk neck to the stem if not planning to string and store in a cool, dry, well-ventilated space or in a basket.

### Onions

• When storing onions, wait for the leaves to begin to flop over or until the tops have completely died away. Then, after a week, use a fork to dig them out of the ground. Lay them out for a few days in the sunlight, or under cover if it is raining. It takes about two weeks until the skins are papery and the

# Storing Crops: Tips

leaves are completely shrivelled. The roots should then be wiry and can be removed. Cut the dead stalk neck to the stem if not planning to string.

- Store strung or in a net in a dry place with good air circulation. Eat thick-necked onions first.

- Store at 2°C to 4°C.

- Note: gasses from the onion can hasten sprouting in potatoes if too close to each other.

**Potatoes**
- Lift the potatoes and brush off excess earth, but do not wash. Finish drying in a sheltered place with plenty of ventilation, then place in a brown paper bag, closed at the neck, and store in a cool, dark, dry place.

- Store at between 5°C to 10°C. If stored below 5°C the starch turns to sugar.

**Squashes**
- A squash is ripe when the stem is hard and wrinkled and difficult to push with your thumbnail. Cut a 'T' shape from the stem and place on a sunny windowsill to cure for two weeks, then store in a dry, airy place. They like a higher temperature and lower humidity than other crops due to their sub-tropical origin.

- Store at a temperature of 10°C to 15°C.

Right: Elephant garlic drying out.

# Storing Crops Record

| Date | Crop type | Location/comment |
| --- | --- | --- |
| | | |
| | | |
| | | |
| | | |
| | | |
| | | |
| | | |
| | | |
| | | |
| | | |
| | | |
| | | |
| | | |
| | | |
| | | |
| | | |
| | | |
| | | |
| | | |
| | | |
| | | |
| | | |
| | | |
| | | |
| | | |

# Storing Crops Record

| Date | Crop type | Location/comment |
|------|-----------|------------------|
|      |           |                  |
|      |           |                  |
|      |           |                  |
|      |           |                  |
|      |           |                  |
|      |           |                  |
|      |           |                  |
|      |           |                  |
|      |           |                  |
|      |           |                  |
|      |           |                  |
|      |           |                  |
|      |           |                  |
|      |           |                  |
|      |           |                  |
|      |           |                  |
|      |           |                  |
|      |           |                  |
|      |           |                  |
|      |           |                  |
|      |           |                  |
|      |           |                  |

# Fresh Flowers

**Early in the morning, when one has just bird song for company, the quiet activity of selecting flowers to bring into the home is one of my greatest pleasures.**

For success, follow these simple guidelines given by professional florists:

- Cut flowers in the early morning, when their stems are full of water and just before they fully open.

- Place stems in a bucket of water immediately and leave in a cool place for a couple of hours for the flowers to drink up lots of water.

- When arranging flowers, cut all the stems at an angle. Remove leaves that will be below the waterline, as they will decompose and hamper water uptake.

- For woody stems like roses, make a 5cm cut upwards from the base of the stem (I find this really fiddly so don't always manage it and the roses don't last as long!).

- Seal stems of flowers that can droop, poppies and hellebores, for example.

- Dip 2.5cm of the stem in just boiled water for 30 seconds before arranging.

- Keep flowers for longer by refreshing a display every couple of days. Change the water and rinse the vase, removing dead flowers or individual flower heads and any dead or dying foliage – check no leaves are below the water line due to shortening stems. Add additional flowers to fill any gaps.

Left: Flowers from the garden for the house.

# Drying Flowers

Drying flowers at the height of their beauty in the middle of summer will give warmth and joy in the middle of winter, when all is gloomy and summer a distant memory.

I remember my mother doing strange things with beech tree branches, bashing their stems with a hammer and soaking them in glycerin. That is a step too far for me, but I do like to dry interesting seed heads and beautiful flowers. They adorn the sitting room on the mantelpiece and around the house through the winter.

There are certain types of flowers that are particularly good for drying, but I like to experiment with what is already in the garden.

Here are a few top tips for drying flowers and foliage:

- Pick the flowers for drying at the correct time, usually in the early morning, as for fresh flowers.
- Choose good-quality flowers with good colour.
- If you need to pick in the rain, shake off any raindrops.
- Prepare for drying as soon as possible, stripping off large leaves.
- Do not remove very small green leaves or attractive grey ones.
- Stiff leaves will dry beautifully, *Echinops*, for example, whose leaves help to keep the flower looking fresh.
- Gather in bunches of about 8-10 stems.

Right: Drying seed heads and flowers.

# Drying Flowers

- Use elastic bands around the stems, as they shrink while drying and elastic will contract with them. String through the band.

- Hang the flowers upside down in a dry space out of direct sunlight, keeping them 6-inch intervals apart.

- I have a horizontal pole and spread flowers across it to dry. Equally effective is to string them vertically with 6-inch gaps between bunches.

- Large flower heads such as artichokes should be tied individually.

- Flowers must be dried as quickly as possible to ensure the colours remain strong. Dry over a boiler, in a hot attic or near some hot pipes, but ensure they have ventilation to allow the moisture to disappear.

- Autumn leaves can be dried by pressing, but I like to iron them. Lay the leaves on blotting paper and use a low heat, ironing directly on the leaf. When totally dry and brittle, coat the leaf with a light paper varnish to make it shine. Floristry wire may be needed to replace the stems.

- Flowers like cornflowers, *Nigella* and lavender need to be picked when in full flower.

- Others, such as *Helichrysum* and *Ammobium,* need to be picked before they're fully open.

Right: Mophead hydrangeas and *Hylotelephium spectabile*, picked for drying.

# Drying Flowers

Flowers and shrubs that retain their scent when dried, such as buddleia 'Black Knight', hyssop, rosemary, lavender, roses and peonies, give an additional pleasure and perfume to a home in winter. I must confess, I struggle with drying roses and peonies, but after buying a dehydrator I have had a lot more success! Herbs with scented flowers and foliage include basil seed heads, calendula and tarragon, when in flower.

Honesty, love-in-a-mist, poppies and teasels all have interesting seed heads. Pick the seed heads when green, making sure the seed pods are well-developed, otherwise they will shrivel. Dried flaxseed has tiny heads, and I pick the whole stem of the plant to add an ethereal bulk to a display. *Acanthus mollis* also provides entertainment in the winter months by shooting its seed pods across the hallway at unsuspecting passers by.

Vegetable flower heads cannot be overlooked: the female varieties of asparagus have orange or scarlet berries and dry well, as do fennel heads and radish seed. Globe artichoke can be picked in flower or as it changes to a seed head – its leaves can be left on. Store dried flowers and seed heads in airtight conditions until wanted for arranging.

I have just listed a few suggestions, but nothing ventured, nothing gained. Gardening is all about experimentation. I have experimented myself with elephant garlic and leek flower heads, picking them just as they come into flower. Displayed without a supporting cast, they create a sculptural simplicity.

# Drying Flowers

I want to give a special mention to my favourite dried flower, mophead hydrangeas. My Instagram interactions show me that people can have problems drying these successfully – pick too early and they will go floppy and fail. Elizabeth Bullivant recommends watching for the real flower in the centre of each large sepal, making sure this has opened and gone over. The mophead should slightly change colour and be firm to the touch. A mophead flower will change colour as the season progresses, so pick according to taste. They will also change colour as they dry.

I put mine in about two inches of water in a vase. When the water is gone, they should be dry in about two weeks, or you can turn them upside down to assist this, as mentioned previously.

## Recommended Reading

**In print**: *Flowers Forever* by Bex Partridge.

**Out of print**: *Dried Fresh Flowers from Your Garden* by Elizabeth Bullivant.

Take notes of your successes and failures in the note section which follows and list any new plants you want to try in the shopping list pages on page 137.

# Dried Flowers Record

| Date | Name | Comment |
|------|------|---------|
|      |      |         |

# Dried Flowers Record

| Date | Name | Comment |
|------|------|---------|
|      |      |         |
|      |      |         |
|      |      |         |
|      |      |         |
|      |      |         |
|      |      |         |
|      |      |         |
|      |      |         |
|      |      |         |
|      |      |         |
|      |      |         |
|      |      |         |
|      |      |         |
|      |      |         |
|      |      |         |
|      |      |         |
|      |      |         |
|      |      |         |
|      |      |         |
|      |      |         |

# Garden Design: Planning

**After being thrown in at the deep end to design an RHS show garden in 2022, winning a silver-gilt medal and the People's Choice Award, as well as a platinum award at BBC Gardeners' World Live 2023, here are some of the things I think about when tackling a garden design project.**

Hard landscaping is costly and difficult to change, so consider getting some professional advice from a landscape gardener or a garden designer. The professional bodies are the Association of Professional Landscapers (APL) and the British Association of Landscape Industries (BALI) and they should be able to point you in the direction of one of their members local to you.

## Assess the Site

- With existing views and background features, look beyond your own border to see if there is anything to enhance your design or that needs screening.

- Be aware of the aspect – which way is the garden or proposed border facing, north, south, east or west?

- Assess the topography, the form and feature of the land's surface. If it's not flat, all the more reason for some professional input!

- See the table on page 96 to work out the light levels: shade, partial shade or sun.

- Check for exposure to wind, extreme heat, frost, footfall pests and children playing.

- Understand your hardiness zone – this is a categorisation description for plants that indicates their suitability for differing climates.

Left: Hampton Court Garden design by Sue Kent.

# Garden Design: Planning

## Testing the Soil

Soil pH is the measure of acidity and alkalinity. Buy a soil pH test strip kit and follow the instructions.

- A pH 6.5 is recommended for gardens, with the exception of lime-hating plants.
- A neutral soil has a pH of 7.0.
- An acid soil has a pH value below 7.0.
- An alkaline soil has a pH value above 7.0.

Once you know, you can check if the plants you want to put into your garden will actually like the soil; if they don't, change the plant selection, don't bother trying to change the soil.

## Water Availability

| Light level categories | Hours of sun per day |
|---|---|
| Sunny | 6+ |
| Half sun, sun/partial shade | 4-6 |
| Shade | 2-4 |
| Dense shade | 0-2 |

# Garden Design: Planning

Identify the soil type – there are lots of online videos to help you work out if it is loam, sand, clay or a mix.

- Establish the soil drainage of your garden: does it hold water or drain well or is it always dry? Is there a structure causing a rain shadow? If so, consider an irrigation system.

- Check the soil depth and observe the health of existing plants and the depth of any existing roots. Will there be competition from large shrub or tree roots for example?

- Based on this assessment of the site you will be able to make good plant choices.

- Research each plant's characteristics, including their size at maturity. The width and height of trees at maturity is very important to get right. Don't be tempted to buy a plant before choosing its location.

- I like to use a spreadsheet to help me select the plants needed. I can then sort it to see if I have interest through the year and complementary colours and shapes of flowers and/or leaf colours and shapes.

- I also need to consider workload – do I want to be lifting and dividing more than I have to? Maybe a different variety has a slower spreading habit and may be a better option. I always check if a plant has toxic sap – as I get close to plants, I need to know, but that is just me!

# Garden Design: Formula and Conversions

Before starting, a wise person measures, and measures again. Costs can ramp up quickly, so planning and costing everything before going ahead, from hard landscaping items to tool hire to plants and soil requirements, is prudent. I always forget formulas and conversions, so I have put in a handy reminder of the things I find useful.

Area = Length × Width

Cubic formula = Length x Width x Height

1 cubic metre = 1000 litres = 35.315 cubic feet

1 square metre = 10.76 square feet

1 millimetre = 0.04 inch

1 centimetre = 0.4 inch

1 metre = 3.28 feet = 1.09 yards

1 kilo = 2.2 pounds

1000 litres = 1 metric tonne

1 imperial ton = 2240 pounds = 1016.05 kilos

1000 kilos = 1 metric tonne = 0.98 imperial ton = 2204.62 pounds

1 Litre = 1.76 pints

4.5 litres = 8 pints = 1 gallon

# Garden Design: Planning

**In this section there are pages for listing plant choices and graph paper to help you plan a new project or a replant of an existing border. Some column headings have been left blank for your requirements. Those I often use are: position, months of interest (to include deciduous, evergreen or dead seed head interest), flowering period and vigour.**

Designing hard landscaping or a new border is great fun, but if you have never done it before it is worth reading up on it before you start. A couple of books that may be helpful are the *RHS Encyclopedia of Garden Design: Planning, Building and Planting your Perfect Outdoor Space* by Chris Young and *How to Create your Garden: Ideas and Advice for Transforming Your Outdoor Space* by Adam Frost.

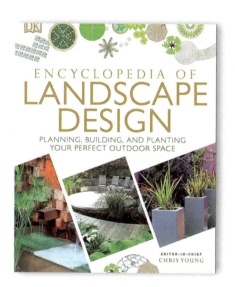
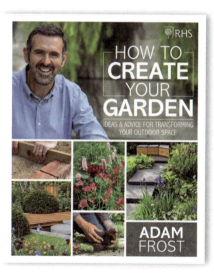

# Garden Design: Plant Selection

| Plant Name | Height | Spread Colour |
| --- | --- | --- |
| | | |
| | | |
| | | |
| | | |
| | | |
| | | |
| | | |
| | | |
| | | |
| | | |
| | | |
| | | |
| | | |
| | | |
| | | |
| | | |
| | | |
| | | |
| | | |
| | | |
| | | |
| | | |
| | | |
| | | |
| | | |

# Garden Design: Plant Selection

# Garden Design: Plant Selection

| Plant Name | Height | Spread Colour |
| --- | --- | --- |
| | | |
| | | |
| | | |
| | | |
| | | |
| | | |
| | | |
| | | |
| | | |
| | | |
| | | |
| | | |
| | | |
| | | |
| | | |
| | | |
| | | |
| | | |
| | | |
| | | |

# Garden Design: Plant Selection

................................................................

_____    _____    _____

_____    _____    _____

_____    _____    _____

_____    _____    _____

_____    _____    _____

_____    _____    _____

_____    _____    _____

_____    _____    _____

_____    _____    _____

_____    _____    _____

_____    _____    _____

_____    _____    _____

_____    _____    _____

_____    _____    _____

_____    _____    _____

_____    _____    _____

_____    _____    _____

# Garden Design: Plant Selection

| Plant Name | Height | Spread Colour |
| --- | --- | --- |
| | | |
| | | |
| | | |
| | | |
| | | |
| | | |
| | | |
| | | |
| | | |
| | | |
| | | |
| | | |
| | | |
| | | |
| | | |
| | | |
| | | |
| | | |
| | | |
| | | |

# Garden Design: Plant Selection

# Garden Design: Grid

# Garden Design: Grid

# Garden Design: Grid

# Garden Design: Grid

# Garden Design: Grid

# Garden Design: Grid

# Garden Design: Grid

# Garden Design: Grid

# Garden Design: Grid

# Garden Design: Grid

# Garden Design: Grid

# Garden Design: Grid

# Garden Design: Notes

# Garden Design: Notes

# Gardener Care

**A garden is a gift for the senses, and becoming aware of the scent, colour, texture and in some cases taste of a plant, together with the sights and sounds of the insect life the plants attract, demands the attention and releases the mind.**

In order to keep our gardens well-maintained, not only do we need to care for our plants and our tools but also keep ourselves in good condition, as gardening can cause muscle aches, pain and injury. As a remedial massage therapist for 15 years, here are my top tips for staying healthy and pain-free.

## Top Tips

Gardeners are at a higher than average risk of skin cancer. I have had it and would like to help you not to. Gardening is absorbing, and before you know it the sun is glaring down and damaging your skin and eyes.

- In summer, try to avoid working when the sun is at its highest and strongest. Wear a sun hat and sunglasses if possible and apply Factor 50 sunscreen before putting a foot outside.

- Avoid dehydration – on hot days, work in a greenhouse or polytunnel only in the early morning and evening, when the sun is not shining directly on them.

- On a cold day, as heat is lost from the top of the head, a warm hat can allow you to garden for longer.

- Wear gloves, long sleeves and glasses when dealing with plants that can cause irritation to the skin and eyes.

Left: Raised bed vegetable gardening.

# Gardener Care

## Warm-up Exercises

- Get your muscles ready for manual work.

- Take both your hands above your head, reaching up to the sky one hand at a time, 10 times in total for each hand to stretch the 'digging' muscles.

- Roll your shoulders forwards and backwards and make large circular movements with your arms to prepare the upper body.

- Swing your arms from side to side and swing your hips in the opposite direction to loosen the lower back.

## Work Well

- Try not to overreach, overbend, or overstretch.

- If there is a big, repetitive job to be done, take a break every 20 minutes or intersperse it with something else requiring a different physical action to prevent repetitive strain.

- When using a lawn mower, steer with two hands and ensure the handle is the correct height so that you are as upright as possible. Mow in straight lines, and don't pull the mower sideways.

### Lifting

- Always lift from a squatting position – don't bend! Use your legs/knees, hold the item close to you and pull in your belly button to activate your abdominal muscles, which will support your back as you come up to standing. Never twist while lifting or putting down. Whenever possible, use a trolley to move heavy items, such as pots or sacks of compost, or use a wheelbarrow, making sure the load is well-balanced.

- Decanting material into lighter loads is also a sensible back-protection technique.

# Gardener Care

**Weeding**
- Weed on your knees for no longer than 20 minutes at a time, as the blood needs to flow through the leg. Try a seated kneeler trolley or a kneeler seat with handles to provide support when returning to a standing position and padding for comfort. Bending forward may cause dizziness, so get up slowly.

**Digging**
- Tools which are long-handled, lightweight and sharp are great to help keep your back straight. Divide digging areas into segments and stop every 20 minutes for a rest and stretch your arms to the sky. By pulling in your belly button when lifting a load on your spade or fork, you contract the abdominal muscles, thereby creating a muscular support around the spine.

- Use smaller trowels and forks – by lifting less weight there is less strain on the wrist. Consider using a garden claw.

- Avoid ladders and overreaching on them, and use long-handled, long-reach loppers or cutters whenever possible.

- Make sure that workbenches and greenhouse staging are the correct height for you to avoid stooping.

# Gardener Care: Five Stretches after Gardening

## 1 Pectoral muscles (used for flexing, rotating and extending the arm)

This stretch is great after using hedge trimmers and long-handled loppers or holding heavy tools up for a period of time. It can be done standing or seated on a stool.

Take your arms behind your back, palms together, then stretch your arms downwards, back and outwards as far as you can and push your chest out, holding for between 30 seconds and 2 minutes. This may help numbness in your hands and wrists, but if it continues after the stretch then get it checked out by a professional.

## 2 Flexor wrists (hand gripping muscles)

If you have been gripping tools for a length of time, for instance during pruning work or using hedge cutters, this is the stretch to do. Stand in front of a wall, an arm's length away. Place your palms flat on the wall, arms straight, hands at shoulder height and shoulder-width apart. Rotate your hands so the fingers are pointing towards the floor, thumbs to the outside, and hold for a minimum of 30 seconds, up to two minutes if tight.

## 3 Piriformis (bottom muscle)

The piriformis rotates the leg during the hip extension and helps keep it in position during flexion of the hip. This muscle can become unhappy after too much digging. Standing on one leg putting pressure through the other can really upset the lower back.

# Gardener Care

If you can alternate your standing leg when digging this would be great, but it is difficult to achieve.

Do this exercise gently and slowly, taking care to get the body straight.

First, sit upright on a chair. Keep your feet on the floor, hip-width apart, toes facing forwards. Lift the left leg and place it over the right knee. Lean forward (don't lean over to the right or left) – you may feel a gentle pull on your lower back and into the left buttock. Don't roll your back, keep it straight and let the weight of you gradually lower over. Hold for a minimum of 30 seconds, up to two minutes. Change over legs and do the same stretch with the right leg crossed over the left knee. You may not be as flexible on one side so stretch more on the tight side. Getting good at this stretch will enable you to keep putting your socks on as you get older.

## 4 Calves

Tightening of the calves can often be caused by a change of footwear, wearing wellies, for example.

Tight calves can cause issues above and below the muscle, giving rise to pain in the knee, hamstring and lower back, as well as the foot. If you only do one exercise, do this one.

Stand in front of a table top or kitchen unit. Place the palms of your hands down flat on a surface with arms straight, shoulder-width apart. Step the left leg back as far as it can go, the heel not quite touching the floor. Keep both hips facing forward. Push through the leg slowly aiming the heel to reach the floor, feel the stretch in the lower leg, stretch for two minutes. If your heel touches the floor, move the leg back slightly and continue. Your leg may be slightly bent to start, but try to get it straight before you finish. Repeat with the other leg.

## 5 Neck retraction

This exercise is helpful if one has been seed sowing or weeding, as it counteracts chronic forward neck posture by strengthening the deep neck flexor muscles.

Stand straight, preferably in front of a mirror, shoulders relaxed and not rotating forward, arms at your sides. Your head shouldn't tip forward or backward. Pull your chin straight backwards as if trying to make a double chin. Do not tip your chin down or upwards at this point. Do not force your head back, aim for 70-80% of your full range of motion. Hold this position for two to three (2-3) seconds, then release your neck back towards neutral position. You should become aware of the muscles contracting at the back of your neck and the centre upper part of your spine.

To help, use your fingers to gently push your chin backwards. When you get the hang of it, use just your neck muscles.

When coming back to neutral from the retracted state, don't stick your chin out past neutral, into a chicken neck posture. Repeat the retraction 20 times, holding for 2-3 seconds each time.

If you experience pain with the exercise, in the future do them more gently, and with less repetitions.

# Tool Care

**Have a specific place for storing garden tools, preferably hanging them up if possible. I am always chanting in my head, 'Don't put it down, put it away.' If this doesn't work, I collect them all up from around the garden at least once a week.**

Do a tool audit before you shop – you can refurbish old tools, and some have multiple uses. For example, a pruning saw can also cleanly divide root-bound plants like mint and erigeron, or a thin trowel for bulb planting can be used to extract weeds with long tap roots. Try tools before buying, assessing weight, length and handle size to make sure they suit your abilities.

## Maintenance

### Wooden-handled tools
• Lightly sand and rub over with linseed oil at the end of the year.

### Spades and forks
• Wipe the handle and shaft then dry it. Brush off soil and dirt from the blade. When it is clean and dry use lubricating oil and paint over the entire blade/tines wiping the excess off.

• Clean cutting tools regularly to avoid spreading disease, let them dry before closing and put them back after use.

Left: Using my favourite tool, a garden claw.

# Tool Care

## Secateurs

I can never remember the correct way to sharpen secateurs, but here are some tips which follow RHS advice and other reputable sources.

- To test the sharpness of secateurs and snips, cut into a sheet of paper – it should cut cleanly and easily. If they are blunt, they will fold and crush the paper rather than cut through it.

- Clean the blade before sharpening to reveal its condition.

- Diamond-coated sharpening blocks or portable pocket-sized tools are ideal for sharpening secateurs and knives on the go. Handheld blade sharpeners generally don't require oil but could have a coarse and fine side, so start with the coarse side.

- Do not sharpen the flat side of the secateurs blade, as this will affect the cutting bite. Sharpen the angled side of the blade only.

- Hold the blade steady and run the diamond tool away from you. Apply even pressure along the blade, including the tip, to expose some new, shiny metal. Try marking the blade with a marker pen before starting – this will be removed as the blade is sharpened and highlight missed sections of blade.

- Buff along the blade in a circular motion with the fine side of the sharpener, finishing with a couple of sweeps in one direction to smooth the metal.

- Put a few drops of general purpose oil or a bit of Vaseline onto the central pivot and spring to improve movement and reduce stiffness.

# My Top Tools

I need tools to help me with many of my garden jobs. Tools are a worthwhile investment, as they enable and empower me in the garden, and I am often asked about those I use. Some are better than others, and where relevant I will name the best brand I have found works for me.

## The large tools

My number one favourite is the **long-handled garden claw**, for removing plants and breaking up compacted soil and aerating compost. The twisting motion can be easier on the back than lifting a fork.

They don't make my favourite one anymore but there are several designs on the market.

When I researched long-handled spades and forks, **Fiskars Xact range long-handled, lightweight fork and spade** seem to be the longest and the lightest. They keep my back at a better angle and provide good leverage. For some reason the handle makes pulling out of the soil easy.

The **Fiscars Xact weed puller** makes removing weeds in the lawn easy and even enjoyable.

I find the standard push-down bulb planter unusable on my stony ground, but the **B&Q long-handled Auger** will normally rotate past the stones and create suitable holes to plant bulbs.

**Auger drill bits** for battery drills are available to make the job even easier (but I am not trusted with a drill!).

# My Top Tools

My husband has a leaf vacuum, which is noisy, requires charging and is too heavy for me, so I tested some leaf grabbers. I found the **Darlac Grab-n-Lift** to be the best so far. It will stay upright on its own and its rubber paddles hug the ground to pick everything up, a brilliant back-protecting and quiet leaf-collection tool.

A **Metal pointed seaside spade** is great for using in raised beds.

A **WOLF-Garten Multi-Change Fruit Collector** makes the task of collecting fallen apples manageable and far less time consuming for me, gathering up many more apples than I could hold in my hands and saving bending and having my nose in the lawn!

Ladders and apple picking are an accident waiting to happen, so I use the **WOLF-Garten Mutlichange Adjustable Fruit Picker** to pick apples from the trees.

**1**. Fiskars Xact weed puller. **2**. Fiskars Xact long-handled spade. **3**. Darlac Grab-n-Lift. **4**. Fiskars Xact long-handled fork. **5**. Seaside spade. **6**. Long-handled garden claw. **7**. WOLF-Garten Multi-Change Fruit Collector.

# My Top Tools

## The Small tools

Secateurs need to be chosen well – quality gives performance. I buy **Okatsune**, which come in three different sizes and are very sharp and effective. I can manage the smaller size, making light work of pruning.

**Garden snips** are good, but small household scissors can work better for me.

For cutting work, the **ARS Long Reach Cut and Hold Pruner** is lightweight with a quality cutting head. Short arms or not, if you need to reach into a border to cut back, this is the ticket.

**A metal-pointed dibber** pushes effortlessly into the soil, making planting seedlings easy.

**Rubber-handled slim trowels and forks** are easier to get a grip and to push into the soil. I select the lightest weight ones I can, which are cheap but seem to last for ages.

**A daisy grubber** is a thin, split-tipped metal weeder tool useful for extracting rooted weeds without disturbing the surrounding soil.

**Dandelion remover**, a slim straight-shafted hand tool that easily goes into the ground. The tip is split to lift the root of the dandelion.

A biro is great for separating small seedlings.

Good-quality plant labels and a marker pen – label well and less mistakes are made!

**8**. ARS Long-Reach Cut and Hold pruner. **9**. Rubber-handled trowel. **10**. Garden snips. **11**. Okatsune secateurs. **12**. Dandelion remover. **13**. Stainless-steel hand dibber. **14**. Daisy grubber. **15**. Garden twine. **16**. Permanent marker. **17**. Plant labels. **18**. Planting Line.

# Shopping Habits

**Watching *BBC Gardeners' World*, I often see a plant I want to have in my garden. The timing may not be right to purchase it, so I jot it down in this section of my garden notebook, together with my thoughts for how and where it will be used, to aid my recall later.**

Obtaining plants for the garden is an exciting prospect. I like to buy bare-rooted trees and plants in winter and spring as it is less expensive and environmentally uses less resources.

The most cost-effective way to grow annuals and perennials is to grow from seed or to take cuttings, but not everyone has the time and space to do this.

Garden catalogues and retailer websites are an inspiration and a temptation. I try not to go plant shopping online or in person without a clear idea of the shape and size of plant I want, and most importantly where I will put it. I have learnt that buying something unplanned for actually causes me stress – I come home and I've got nowhere to put it and give myself more work!

Using a local nursery can mean the plants are locally grown and a good indicator they will do well in the area. A local good nursery can provide a wealth of plant knowledge and advice.

Larger garden centres are great for inspiration and have plants at their peak performance time, so there is no expectation gap when making a purchase.

There are lots of things to consider when buying plants, and the RHS have a great guide on what to look for. I recommend visiting the link below and having a good read before any plant purchases.

**www.rhs.org.uk/garden-design/buying-garden-plants**

# Shopping List

**Item**

# Shopping List

**Item**

# Shopping List

**Item**

# Gift Ideas for Gardeners

**Gardeners are a practical bunch and we love practical useful gifts.**

If you've got long-term gardening friends, it's useful to keep a record of what you've given them, and in this book you can do just that. I have been gardening for 35 years and have had quite a few Christmases and birthdays packed with gardening gifts, so here are a few of my favourite things.

## Easy-on-the-pocket presents

- For first-time gardeners, a trowel, a fork, a bucket and a sweeping brush are a good place to start.
- Garden twine, the bigger the ball the better.
- Plastic plant labels and a permanent marker pen. Plastic is not ideal, but nothing else works as well – they eventually fade and can be reused.
- A Dibber – they come in lots of sizes.
- Support canes.
- A split-pronged weeding fork.
- A lightweight watering can – it does not have to be plastic, there are nice lightweight metal ones on Amazon.
- Liquid plant food.
- Gardening gloves (obviously not for me).
- Packets of seeds that can be sown directly into the soil and reliably come up.
- Packets of bulbs.
- Kneeling pad.

# Gift Ideas for Gardeners

- Factor 50 sunscreen.
- A nail brush and hand cream.
- Gardening books (see page 147 for recommendations).
- I don't tend to buy people plants unless I know they really want them.

## A little more money to spend?

- Garden tools are an investment – check out all my favourite ones on page 130.
- Investing in an expensive pair of secateurs is well worth it – one can never have too many pairs.
- Long-handled pruners and loppers.
- A trug.
- A heated propagator – this item can take up quite a lot of space, so might not be appropriate, but there are different sizes available.
- A cold frame, as above.
- Terracotta pots.
- Weeding stool/trolley.

# Gift Ideas for Gardeners

## Clothing

- A wax jacket to prevent getting tangled up in your plants.

- Rose pruning gloves.

- Genus gardening clothing, specifically designed for gardening to avoid sore and wet knees, damp bottoms and cold backs. You can't go wrong with something from this range.

- Poddy and Black half-cut boots/shoes are easier to put on than wellingtons.

## Something easy to post

Memberships and subscriptions stay in the receiver's memory and are an easy gift to send or give in person. Here are a few suggestions. The list is by no means comprehensive.

## Memberships

- Many large, privately owned gardens have an annual membership with benefits.

- Membership of the Royal Horticultural Society includes access to discounted show tickets and entry to their five gardens. Within the package is an excellent monthly magazine, *The Garden*.
  **www.rhs.org.uk**

- Membership of the National Trust brings with it 180 registered parks and gardens, the largest collection of historic gardens and parks in Europe.
  **www.nationaltrust.org.uk**

# Gift Ideas for Gardeners

- A subscription to Garden Organic helps to promote and fight for environmental matters. Included is access to a wealth of organic scientific information database and *The Organic Life* magazine, published three times a year. **www.gardenorganic.org.uk**

## Magazine Subscriptions

- *BBC Gardeners' World* magazine is full of clear, well-illustrated guidance and often includes free seeds and discounts on garden visits and for online retailers. **www.gardenersworld.com**

- *Gardens Illustrated* magazine is a pictorial feast focused on remarkable gardens, plants and design. **www.gardensillustrated.com**

- *Kitchen Garden* magazine is all about growing your own fruits and vegetables. **www.kitchengarden.co.uk**

- *Garden News* is a weekly magazine full of the latest plant news and practical advice. **www.gardennewsmagazine.co.uk**

- *The English Garden* magazine illustrates traditional and modern gardens and offers gardening advice. **www.theenglishgarden.telegraph.co.uk**

# Gift Record

| Gift name | Date | Receiver |
|-----------|------|----------|
|           |      |          |
|           |      |          |
|           |      |          |
|           |      |          |
|           |      |          |
|           |      |          |
|           |      |          |
|           |      |          |
|           |      |          |
|           |      |          |
|           |      |          |
|           |      |          |
|           |      |          |
|           |      |          |
|           |      |          |
|           |      |          |
|           |      |          |
|           |      |          |
|           |      |          |
|           |      |          |
|           |      |          |

COLLINS

side Gardening
Bullingbridge

Isabel Bannerman

VEG IN ON
aniel J. inkley
Wi
Macunovich        Easy Gard
DESIGN IN THE GARDEN    U Barth
JOHN BROOKES    GARDEN
DREAM PLANTS FOR THE NATUR
GARDEN STYL
FLOWER GARDEN
Austin  Levy  Ued  BAMBO

THE HOSTA BOOK
MAKING THE MOST OF CLEMATIS
Shrubs    Roger Phillips & Martyn Rix
The Bulb Book    Martyn Rix & Roger Phillips
Perennials    VOLUME I EARLY PERENNIALS
Perennials    VOLUME 2 LATE PERENNIALS
No Dig Organic Home & Garden
Peter Beales    CLASSIC ROS
The Duchess of Beaufort's Flowers
FROST
THE NAMING OF N
Paul Ad

# Gardening Books

**Although the Internet and social media provide great gardening resources, I have discovered through the years that there is nothing like reading a book to really develop one's knowledge and understanding of the subject.**

Gardening books come in many guises: there is the how-to book, which hopefully does what it says on the cover and tells you how to do the thing you're looking to do; there are the history of gardening books and profiles of famous gardens and gardeners; there are books on specific gardening styles, like cottage gardening or Japanese gardening; there are books on specific plant types, like roses or irises; and there are science-based books filled with experiments and test results – I rather like these because I love theories being put to the test.

On my website is my second-hand garden bookshop. Many of the books listed are no longer in print but make for interesting reading. Some are quite eye-opening due to their lust for chemical cures for every pest and disease (I'm so glad we've moved away from that), and some are stunningly beautiful, capturing gardens from another time in their prime.

The books I enjoy the most are gardening stories, taking the reader right into that person's gardening life, and through which so many interesting thoughts and lessons are shared.

Here are some of the books I have enjoyed, some of which are out of print but can be bought online. In this section of the notebook there is space for you to list books you would like or those you have read and would like to recommend to fellow gardening enthusiasts.

# Gardening Books: Good Reads

## Reference Books

*The RHS Encyclopedia of Plants and Flowers* by Christopher Bricknell

## How to

*RHS Pruning* by Christopher Bricknell

*Veg in One Bed* by Huw Richards

*No Dig Organic, Home and Garden: Grow, Cook, Use & Store Your Harvest* by Charles Dowding and Stephanie Hafferty

## Gardening Stories

*Windcliff* by Daniel J. Hinkley

*Plot 29: A Love Affair with Land* by Allan Jenkins

*The Curious Gardener* by Anna Pavord

*The Well-Tempered Garden* by Christopher Lloyd (out of print)

*Husbandry* by Isabel Bannerman

## Science

*The Woodchip Handbook* by Ben Raskin

*The Regenerative Growers Guide to Garden Amendments* by Nigel Palmer

## Garden Design

*Easy Garden Design* by Janet Macunovich (out of print)

## Plant Books

*Dream Plants for the Natural Garden* by Henk Gerritsen and Peit Oudolf (out of print)

*Best Climbers* by Stefan Buczacki (out of print)

. . . . . . . . . . . . . . . . . . . . . . . .

On my list to be purchased (I asked for Christmas and birthday but was unlucky):

*The Grove: A Nature Odyssey in 19 ½ Front Gardens* by Ben Dark

Browse my second-hand book shop: **www.suekent.com/shop**.

# Gardening Books: Reading List

# Gardening Books: Reading List

# Visiting Gardens

**One can get so caught up in one's own garden with all the jobs that need to be done that visiting other gardens can fall down the priority list. I holiday with my husband in the UK, and this is when we manage to squeeze in a few garden visits. I find these very stimulating and thought-provoking, and some of the lessons I have taken from them have shaped my own garden.**

- In Wales, Aberglasney in Carmarthenshire gave me an education of colour in shade, and Powis Castle in Welshpool inspired me to terrace my unmanageable bank of shrubs!

- The National Trust garden in Cliveden at present has two very large herbaceous borders, one planted with cool colours and one with hot colours. Being able to observe colour displayed in this way allows the visitors to explore how these colours make them feel and what colours suit them. Cool colours suit me!

- The Hauser & Wirth garden in Somerset by Piet Oudolf, if visited in winter, illustrates the beauty of perennials in their decayed state and offers an alternative blonde vista to the traditional evergreen in the English winter garden.

- David Austin Roses have show gardens near Wolverhampton to display all manner of ways of using roses within the garden.

- The Alnwick Garden in Northumberland is a brilliant contemporary garden with a highly educative poisonous plants garden tour. The knowledge I gained there saved me from my thalictrums.

Left: Aberglasney Gardens, Carmarthenshire.

# Visiting Gardens

- Trebah in Cornwall block plant hydrangeas in their wooded valley. This was inspirational for me, and I went on to create a 40-foot hydrangea border in my garden.

- Garden Organic's demonstration garden at Ryton is packed with ideas for organic vegetable growing.

- The National Garden Scheme provides inspiration every year by opening up over 3,500 gardens, big and small. Visit **www.ngs.org.uk** for up-to-date information.

- The RHS has five gardens to visit, while the National Trust has many more, all listed on their website.

- Garden shows which feature show gardens can also be very useful, with lots of take-home hard landscaping and planting ideas. The shows also have specialist growers who understand if the plants you're tempted to buy are suitable for your growing conditions.

When travelling abroad in the past, I loved visiting gardens. Although often the climate is different, the style and design in another country can give pause for thought and open up lines of creativity once back home.

This notebook has space to write down the names of gardens you read about in the media or those that friends recommend. It may be useful to note garden show dates also, keeping all this useful visiting list in one place.

Right: Trebah Garden, Cornwall.

# Gardens to Visit

| Garden name | Location | Comment |
|---|---|---|
| | | |
| | | |
| | | |
| | | |
| | | |
| | | |
| | | |
| | | |
| | | |
| | | |
| | | |
| | | |
| | | |
| | | |
| | | |
| | | |
| | | |
| | | |
| | | |
| | | |
| | | |
| | | |

# Gardens to Visit

| Garden name | Location | Comment |
| --- | --- | --- |
|  |  |  |
|  |  |  |
|  |  |  |
|  |  |  |
|  |  |  |
|  |  |  |
|  |  |  |
|  |  |  |
|  |  |  |
|  |  |  |
|  |  |  |
|  |  |  |
|  |  |  |
|  |  |  |
|  |  |  |
|  |  |  |
|  |  |  |
|  |  |  |
|  |  |  |

# Address Book

| Supplier name | Location | Comment |
| --- | --- | --- |
| | | |
| | | |
| | | |
| | | |
| | | |
| | | |
| | | |
| | | |
| | | |
| | | |
| | | |
| | | |
| | | |
| | | |
| | | |
| | | |
| | | |
| | | |
| | | |
| | | |
| | | |
| | | |
| | | |
| | | |
| | | |

# About The Author

**Sue Kent is an award-winning gardening television presenter and an RHS Ambassador for disability. Having 8" arms and only 7 fingers and no thumbs, she uses both her feet and small hands to garden.**

Sue comes at gardening from an angle new to many of us but one that is also completely relatable. She connects immediately with audiences through her infectious enthusiasm for the subject and zest for life, helping them gain a greater understanding of how they can unlock their own abilities through design and plant choices while protecting environmental resources and wildlife.

She has lived in Wales for over 30 years in her house by the sea, where her large garden has four different levels sheltered by cliffs and woodland. Six years ago she also took on an organic allotment to develop her fruit and vegetable growing capacity.

In the last couple of years Sue has ventured into the world of show garden design, receiving an RHS silver-gilt medal and *Gardeners' World Live* platinum award.

**www.suekent.com**

*Sue Kent: Garden Notes*, first published in Great Britain in 2023 by Graffeg Limited.

Text by Sue Kent, copyright © 2023.
Designed and produced by Graffeg Limited, copyright © 2023.

Graffeg Limited, 24 Stradey Park Business Centre, Mwrwg Road, Llangennech, Llanelli, Carmarthenshire, SA14 8YP, Wales, UK. www.graffeg.com.

ISBN 9781802585889

1 2 3 4 5 6 7 8 9

Photography: © Alamy: Pages 152, 155.
© Jenny Smith Photography: Pages 4, 159.
© Sue Kent: Pages 10, 50, 78, 89, 94.
© Shutterstock: Pages 3, 45
All other photography © Jason Ingram.

Right: *Agapanthus*.

Overleaf: *Nigella damascena* and poppy seed heads.